GARFIELD

Look What's Brewing!

In the olden days, those guys who dressed like Wee Willie Winkie were always trying to turn base metals into gold. Well, I've done it! Being the megastar that I am, I've turned the humble Christmas annual into a book the whole world wants to read. The fourth Garfield Annual is a classic that can be treasured alongside Jane Eyre, Oliver Twist and The Good Pizza Guide.

Here are the ingredients –
- 4 brand new stories all about me.
- 20 pages of comic strips all about me.
- 2 great feature articles both about me.
- 3 bound-in posters with pictures of me.
- A brill knitting pattern that makes a cushion with me on it.
- A quiz about home, the place I love best.
- 2 special puzzles cleverly devised by me.
- Some other stuff with kittens, Arlene, Jon and Odie which I mention to show how modest I am.

Mixed together, these ingredients will produce laughter that lasts longer than a snooker tournament on TV. This annual is a perfect blend of humour, wit and intelligence (all mine) that will stand the test of time. Like I say of lasagne: "A thing of beauty is a joy for supper."

GARFIELD
ANNUAL

Created by
JiM DAViS

Written by
Gordon Volke

RAVETTE BOOKS

CONTENTS

Pussy Cat, Pussy Cat, Where Have You Been? .... page 7
Garfield Strips 11
Home Sweet Home 16
Garfield's Cushy Number 18
Bound-in Poster 20
A Tale Of Two Kitties 21
Cute Kittens 24
Garfield's Traditional Dish Puzzle 26
Garfield Strips 27
Bound-in Poster 32
Arlene's Arroword 34
Look Who's Talking 35
Odie's Spiral Puzzle 38
Garfield Strips 39
A Dog Called Garfield 44
Garfield On Stage 46
Jon's Dot-To-Dot Quiz 48
Bound-in Poster 50
Garfield Strips 51
Garfield's Coded Joke 56
A Cuckoo In The Ness 57
Answers 61

Copyright © 1992 United Feature Syndicate, Inc. All Rights Reserved. Published by Ravette Books Limited 1992.

Printed and bound for Ravette Books Limited, 3 Glenside Estate, Star Road, Partridge Green, Horsham, West Sussex RH13 8RA, an Egmont company, by STIGE, Italy.

ISBN: 1 85304 422 9

PUSSY CAT, PUSSY CAT, WHERE HAVE YOU BEEN?

Picturepoint – London

Garfield and Jon were visiting London.

"Let's do the sights," said Jon.

"Let's do lunch," said Garfield.

"Where do you fancy?" mused Jon. "The Houses of Parliament? Nelson's Column? Madame Tussaud's?"

"Are they in the Good Food Guide?" asked Garfield.

"I know!" cried Jon. "Buckingham Palace! We can watch the changing of the guard!"

"I'm not Christopher Robin," yawned Garfield.

"And there's a Garden Party on this afternoon. We can watch the guests arriving in their top hats and tails."

Garfield brightened visibly at this news.

"I can go to the party," he grinned. "I've got a tail!"

As soon as they reached the Palace, Garfield marched right up to the gates. He was met by a stern-looking sentry.

"Never mind all the 'friend or foe' stuff," said Garfield, "point me in the direction of the grub!"

The sentry just prodded Garfield with his rifle until he was out on the pavement again.

"You need a special invitation to attend the party, Garfield," explained Jon.

"Is that so?" muttered Garfield. "Mine must have been lost in the post."

The thought of a delicious party spread made Garfield feel hungrier than ever. He left Jon taking photographs of the soldiers and wandered off on his own, peering at the gutter.

"The corgis might have thrown out a bone," he mumbled.

Suddenly, an open-top carriage clattered past and a piece of paper blew out of the gloved hand of one of the occupants. It somersaulted through the air and landed at Garfield's feet. He picked it up and a grin the size of the Grand Canyon spread across his face.

"Just the ticket!" he chuckled.

Garfield stomped back to the Palace gates. Jon was still busy with his camera, so he marched straight up to the scowling sentry and waved the piece of paper under his nose.

"It says 'ADMIT ONE', buddy boy!" grinned Garfield.

The soldier gave a respectful salute and indicated a nearby cloakroom. Garfield hurried inside and emerged a few moments later with a top hat, a cane, a dicky-bow and some smart cuffs. He charged towards the garden.

"Let's party!" he yelled.

While other guests waited for the Queen to appear (Her Majesty was late coming out for some reason), Garfield powered his way through the food. It was set out on long tables covered with white cloths and Garfield found it quickest to tip up each table and let the smoked salmon sandwiches and strawberry tarts slide down into his mouth.

"I'll leave a couple of vol-au-vents," he thought. "It's manners."

After his feast, Garfield felt extremely tired.

"I'll mosey indoors for a nap," he yawned.

Garfield wandered the corridors looking for somewhere to sleep. He found a comfy cushion at one end of a big room and was just closing his eyes when he heard a shriek from the other side of a tall silk screen.

"Someone turn the TV down," he muttered.

It was followed by a second scream which sent Garfield scurrying to investigate. He found a well-dressed lady standing on a footstool, pointing fearfully to a chair in the corner. There was a mouse underneath it!

Garfield recognised the lady at once.

"This is a job for Mouse-busters, Maam," he said.

Garfield strode over and wagged his thumb at the mouse.

"On your bike," he ordered.

"Get lost," replied the mouse. "You're no mouser!"

"My reputation precedes me," sighed Garfield. "Suppose I asked you very politely if you'd be kind enough to move along?"

"I like it here," said the mouse, folding his arms.

"I'll let you cuddle my teddy," offered Garfield.

"How infantile!" exclaimed the mouse.

"You can watch my video of Binky the Clown," cried Garfield.

"Who?" asked the mouse.

At this point, Garfield made a grab for the mouse who sidestepped neatly and retreated further under the chair. He stuck his tongue out at Garfield and blew a loud raspberry.

"Rule 27 of the Troublesome Rodent Handbook," murmured Garfield. "STAY COOL!"

Garfield pretended to look out of the window.

"PSST!" he whispered behind his hand. "There's a big do out in the garden. Some greedy oaf scoffed all the grub, so they've brought in loads more. You don't know what you're missing."

The mouse shot out from his hiding place faster than a sprinter in an Olympic final.

"Thanks to Odie," smiled Garfield, "I have years of experience at manipulating the lower orders."

Meanwhile, outside the railings, Jon was becoming increasingly anxious about his pet.

"Where can Garfield have got to?" he exclaimed.

Jon tried asking an equally worried-looking man in a top hat and gloves, but the gentleman was not prepared to help.

"I've lost my invitation to the Garden Party," he cried.

Just then, there was a fanfare of trumpets and two footmen appeared, unrolling a red carpet.

"Someone very important must be coming out," gasped Jon.

There was a hushed silence as everyone waited for the VIP to appear. Then Garfield wandered out of the Palace and strolled down the carpet, carrying a big box of chocolates in one hand and waving goodbye with the other.

"Garfield!" exclaimed Jon. "Where have you been?"

"I've been to London to visit the Queen," crowed Garfield.

"What did you get up to in the Palace?" cried Jon.

"Don't feed me that line, bird-brain!" snapped Garfield. "How can I make it rhyme?"

Garfield marched straight past Jon and handed his ticket to the anxious-looking gentleman.

"If you nip in quick," he said, "you might still get some afters."

Jon stared curiously at the box of chocolates which Garfield opened and started to eat.

"And what are those?" he asked.

"Royalties," replied Garfield.

RATS, WHAT HAPPENED TO THE MAPLE SYRUP?

NOW I REMEMBER... THE SYRUP BOTTLE SPRANG A LEAK

10-4

SO I POURED IT IN JON'S HAIR TONIC BOTTLE

JIM DAVIS

THIS HAS POSSIBILITIES

JIM DAVIS 10-6

JIM DAVIS 10-7

DRIVE-THRU RESTAURANTS ARE SO CONVENIENT

GIMME THAT!

I HAVE PLANS FOR THIS RADIO CONTROLLED TANK

WE'LL TAKE NO PRISONERS

HOW CUTE. A TOY TANK

SORRY ABOUT THAT. BUT, WE HAD REASON TO BELIEVE YOUR TUNA CASSEROLE WAS LEAKING TROOP MOVEMENT INFORMATION TO THE ENEMY

ALL YOU NEED IS SHOVE!

MUNCH
CHOMP
GULP

JUST WHEN YOU THOUGHT IT WAS SAFE TO HAVE BREAKFAST...

AS THE SHARK APPROACHES HIS PREY, HE SENSES SOMETHING AMISS

OH, YEAH. WATER! SHARKS NEED WATER!

SELF-INDULGENCE

THERE'S A MESSAGE IN THOSE GREAT WORDS

IF YOU DON'T INDULGE YOURSELF... NOBODY WILL

HEY, GARFIELD, DO YOU KNOW WHAT TIME IT IS?

LUNCH TIME?

IT'S TIME FOR FUN WITH STATIC ELECTRICITY!

THE MAN IS A LAUGH RIOT

15

HOME SWEET HOME

Are you a home-loving bird like Garfield? (Don't glare like that, Garfield – just a figure of speech!) Why not find out by tackling this quiz all about houses and homes.
Answers on page 61.

1. Can you complete this well-known saying?
'Home is where the – – – – – is.'

2. Which bird has a home called an eyrie?
(a) Golden eagle
(b) Silver spookbird
(c) Barn owl

3. Which mammal has a home called a holt?
(a) Otter
(b) Scottish wildcat
(c) Blue whale

4. Who lived at 21a Baker Street?

5. Who lived at Camelot?

6. The Prime Minister lives at 10 Downing Street, but who lives at number 11?
(a) The Queen
(b) The Deputy Prime Minister
(c) The Chancellor of the Exchequer

7. Where, in Greek legend, was the home of the gods?
(a) Mount Vesuvius
(b) Mount Olympus
(c) Mount Everest

8. Can you match these six famous football teams with their home grounds?

Liverpool	White Hart Lane
Tottenham Hotspur	Old Trafford
Arsenal	The Dell
Manchester United	Highbury
Leeds	Anfield
Southampton	Elland Road

9. What is the popular name for the Home Guard of the Second World War?
(a) Dad's Army
(b) Mum's Army
(c) Ministry of Defence

10. Can you complete this sentence?
"Tribes with no fixed homeland who wander from place to place with their cattle are called – – – – – –."

11. What is the difference between a rabbit burrow and a rabbit warren?

12. Which king first built the Tower of London?
(a) William the Conqueror
(b) Henry the Eighth
(c) George the Fifth

13. Which king first built Hampton Court Palace?
(a) William the Conqueror
(b) Henry the Eighth
(c) George the Fifth

14. Who made his home on a desert island as a result of being shipwrecked?

15. According to the nursery rhyme, where did the person live who had so many children she didn't know what to do?

16. Who lived for a while with a gang of pickpockets in Victorian London?

17. 'Heimat' is the Spanish word for 'home'.
(a) True?
(b) False?

18. Which animal lives in a set (or sett)?
(a) Weasel
(b) Badger
(c) Hare

19. New Zealand is the homeland of the aboriginees.
(a) True?
(b) False?

20. Who lives next door to Garfield and Jon?
(a) Hubert and Reba
(b) Nermal
(c) Doc Boy

Garfield's Cushy Number

Calling all you Garfield knit-wits! Here's a simple pattern designed by knitting expert, Joy Gammon, which makes a colourful Garfield cushion, or framed picture, or both. So get out those needles and start clicking (or, alternatively, smile sweetly at your mum or gran!)

MATERIALS

READICUT Wharfedale Double Knitting in:

For the Cushion:
Bright green (1120) 2 balls
Darker blue (1114) 2 balls
Bright yellow (1110) small quantity
PLUS, 16½in cushion pad or equivalent stuffing.

For the Picture:
Paler blue (1128) 1 ball
Aqua (2706) 1 ball
Pale yellow (1127) small quantity
PLUS, a picture frame up to 16in sq. (41cm sq.)

PLUS, for each item:
small quantities of orange (1119), black (1108), pink (1126), white (1113), and pale yellow (1127).

TENSION

22 sts and 30 rows=10cm (4in) in st.st. on 4mm (No. 8) needles.

4mm needles and st.st. are used throughout.

KEY TO CHART & PATTERN

For the CUSHION
G =bright green
Y1 =bright yellow
BL=darker blue (1114)
Y2 =pale yellow

For the PICTURE
G =aqua   BL=paler blue (2719)
Y1 =pale yellow Y2 =pale yellow

For each item
O=orange. B=black. P=pink.
W=white.
– – – =embroidery lines.
×=additional black sts.
⇑ = edges of work.

CUSHION FRONT or PICTURE

Using G, cast on 91 sts and, starting with a K row, work 32 rows. Commence working from the chart on the next row, placing it as given.

Cont. until all 69 rows of the chart have been worked.
Work a further 23 rows in BL.
Cast off loosely.
Press according to ball band instructions.
Using the chart and picture as a guide, embroider detail.

CUSHION BACK

Using G, cast on 91 sts and work 71 rows.
Change to BL and work a further 53 rows.
Cast off loosely.
Press according to ball band instructions

TO MAKE UP CUSHION

back and front together around three sides matching colours. Insert cushion or stuffing and close remaining side.

TO MAKE UP PICTURE – Frame as preferred.

GARFIELD CUSHION/PICTURE   CENTRE ST.

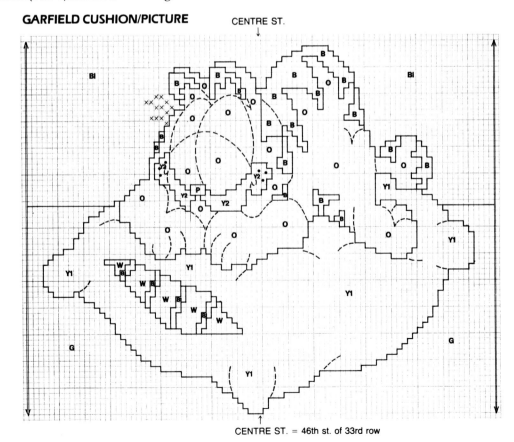

CENTRE ST. = 46th st. of 33rd row

18

AND THERE'S MORE!

If you have enjoyed this pattern, there
are lots more exciting designs in
The Garfield Knitting Book.

A TALE OF TWO KITTIES

"Guess what, Garfield," cried Nermal, marching excitedly in through the door. "You're emigrating to Outer Mongolia?" exclaimed Garfield. "You've taken poison? You're going to play marbles on the motorway?"
"There's a Cute Kitten Contest being held by the Healthy Eating Society," explained Nermal, "and I'm favourite to win."
"Colour me totally unimpressed," yawned Garfield.
    Nermal sat beside Garfield's bed, fluttering his eyelids prettily. Garfield lay inside, keeping his eyes tight shut in the hope that Nermal would go away.
"Pity you can't enter the Contest, Garfield," sighed Nermal. "You're too old . . ."
"I'm not old," interrupted Garfield. "I'm more over-young."
". . . and fat," continued Nermal.
"I'm not fat, either," retorted Garfield, "I'm just under-tall."
Nermal began to snigger, so Garfield lashed out with his paw. But the kitten was too nimble. He skipped aside and sauntered out through the door.
"You wouldn't win anyway, Garfield," called Nermal. "You don't know the meaning of 'cute'!"

As Nermal went out of one door, Jon came in through another.

"Did you miss me, Garfield?" he said. "I've been visiting my folks down on the farm."

"You have such charisma, I didn't even know you'd gone," murmured Garfield.

"Great-Granny Arbuckle was there, Garfield," continued Jon. "She's an *amazing* woman! She climbs mountains, runs marathons and takes part in professional wrestling – all at the age of 104!"

"Remind me never to meet her," muttered Garfield.

"*And,*" added Jon, taking a little bottle out of his pocket, "she attributes it all to this – her special homemade tonic. She says it gives her Eternal Youth!"

"Tonics give me Eternal YEUCH!" growled Garfield.

This tonic proved to be different. When Jon popped the cork, a delicious smell of freshly baked lasagne filled the room.

"Great-Granny made it especially for you," explained Jon.

Garfield grabbed the old-fashioned bottle and tipped the contents down his throat.

"Not bad," remarked Garfield. "A little on the heavy side, but then so am I."

"How do you feel now, Garfield?" asked Jon, eagerly.

"Tired," yawned Garfield.

"Don't you feel rejuvenated and energetic?" cried Jon.

"Get real," said Garfield, shaking his head.

"I give up!" groaned Jon.

Jon went out again.

"Guess he's looking for his personality," thought Garfield, settling down for a quiet, two-day nap. Suddenly, he began to feel peculiar.

"Has Arlene come into the room?" he cried. "I've gone all light-headed!"

Garfield found himself growing smaller – something he had never known in his life before. When he looked in the mirror, he saw he had turned into a kitten.

"Must be that stuff!" he gasped.

Garfield scampered upstairs. (It was very difficult because they were now so big.) He rooted through some old clothes until he found a bow-tie, a bonnet and some matching rompers. He put them on.

"'Cute' doesn't even come into it," he grinned.

A short while later, in the local hall, Nermal lined up with the other kittens for the judging of the Contest. He looked calm and confident.

"It's easy when you're beautiful," he cooed.

Suddenly, the public-address system crackled into life.

"Your attention, ladies and gentlemen," said the announcer. "There has been a last-minute entry in the competition. Contestant number 11 is just taking his place now."

Nermal's eyes grew as round as saucers as a familiar orange figure, several times smaller than usual, sauntered past in baby clothes, giving an appealing smile.

"It c-c-can't be!" exclaimed Nermal.

"It *is*, punk," growled Garfield.

The Contest was over from that moment on. Garfield won first prize, beating Nermal into a humiliating second place.

"You cheated!" protested the outraged kitten.

"You sure look cute when you're angry," laughed Garfield, "but not as cute as me. Look what I can do with this ball of wool!" Garfield lay on his back and rolled the ball in his paws. Then he flipped it into the air so it landed on Nermal's head.

"I love adding insult to injury," sniggered Garfield.

Suddenly, Garfield began to feel light-headed again. He fled from the Contest like Cinderella from the ball.

"Send my prize on," he called, indicating a large box with a ribbon wrapped round it. By the time he reached home, Garfield had returned to normal.

A few days later, the box arrived.
Garfield rubbed his paws with glee.
"Wonder what's inside?"
he giggled. "Toys? Chocolate?
Lasagne?"

Like a shark in a feeding-frenzy. Garfield tore open the box and out poured an avalanche of raisins. Garfield snatched up the slip that accompanied them. 'With compliments of the Healthy Eating Society', it said.

"WAAH!" yelled Garfield.

When Jon came into the room, he found Garfield leaping around banging his head on the walls and pulling out pawfuls of fur.

"For goodness sake, Garfield," he cried, "act your age!"

CUTE KITTENS

These are the other contestants in the
Cute Kitten Contest . . .

Picturepoint – London

Picturepoint – London

Picturepoint – London

RUNNERS UP

RUNNER UP

RUNNERS UP

Picturepoint – London

Picturepoint – London

25

Garfield's Traditional Dish Puzzle

Here are a dozen world-famous foods, all of which Garfield has eaten (at one sitting!) Can you connect each food with its country of origin? The first one has been done for you.
Answers on page 61.

PIZZA	FRANCE
PAELLA	JAPAN
HAGGIS	INDIA
CHOP SUEY	SPAIN
SNAILS	GERMANY
CURRY	ENGLAND
MOUSSAKA	SCOTLAND
FISH AND CHIPS	GREECE
CHILLI CON CARNE	AMERICA
SUSHI (Raw Fish)	MEXICO
HAMBURGERS	ITALY
SAUERKRAUT	CHINA

SQUEEZE

HA, HA, HA! YOU SQUEEZED POOKY TOO HARD HUH? THAT'S HYSTERICAL!

SQUEEZE

SQUEEZE

ARRRGH!

GOOD NEWS, GARFIELD

I COMPLETELY RESTUFFED POOKY FOR YOU

ARLENE'S ARROWORD

Arlene has been stood up by Garfield more times than a chair with one leg. To pass the time, she thinks up crosswords – *very* cross words for Garfield and cunning crosswords like this! Solve the clues and write your answers in the grid in the direction indicated by the arrows. Solution on page 61.

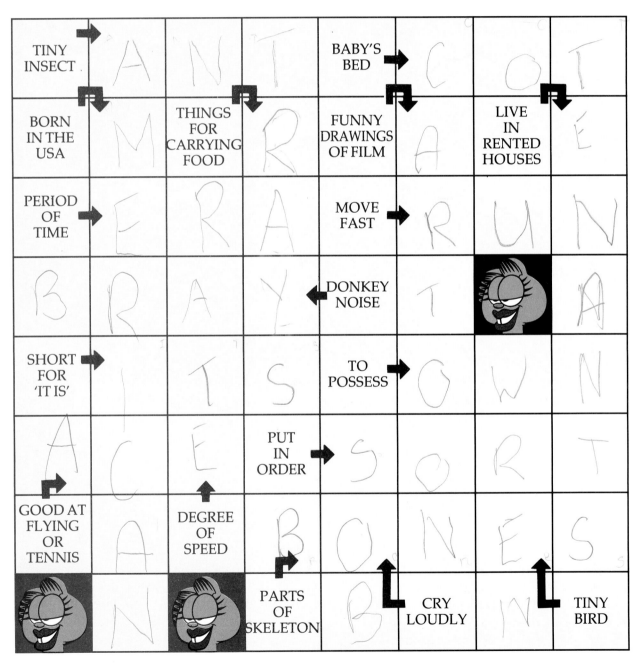

TINY INSECT			BABY'S BED		LIVE IN RENTED HOUSES
BORN IN THE USA	THINGS FOR CARRYING FOOD		FUNNY DRAWINGS OF FILM		
PERIOD OF TIME			MOVE FAST		
		DONKEY NOISE			
SHORT FOR 'IT IS'			TO POSSESS		
		PUT IN ORDER			
GOOD AT FLYING OR TENNIS	DEGREE OF SPEED			CRY LOUDLY	TINY BIRD
		PARTS OF SKELETON			

LOOK WHO'S TALKING

"To beat up or not to beat up? That is the question," said Garfield, pacing backwards and forwards. It was a cold, wet day and Garfield was bored, bored, bored. Jon had gone out, there was nothing interesting on TV and Garfield had already eaten every scrap of food in the house.

"What else is there to do except beat up Odie?" he sighed.

The trouble was, Garfield felt an occasional pang of guilt about being so mean to his best friend, particularly as Odie was always so loyal.

"I have a feeling I might get my come-uppance one day," said Garfield.

At that moment, Odie bounded into the room. He gave an excited bark.

"You want to play, Odie?" said Garfield. "Okay, let's have a game of spinning tops."

Odie put his head on one side and whined anxiously.

"I know we haven't got a spinning top, Odie," continued Garfield. "So we'll have to use *you* instead."

Garfield grabbed hold of Odie's tongue and wound it round his body. Then he gave a sharp tug and sent Odie spinning across the room like a miniature whirlwind.

"I can resist everything except temptation," quipped Garfield.

Odie whizzed across the room and collided head-first with the wall.

"Are you okay, Odie?" asked Garfield.

"I t-t-think so," replied the dog.

"Shall we do it again, then?" cried Garfield.

"Noooo," wailed Odie.

Suddenly, Garfield stopped in his tracks.

"There's something wrong here!" he exclaimed. He inspected his stomach, but that was its usual size. The room looked normal. There was one leaf left on Jon's fern, but that was not it. Then it dawned on Garfield.

"Odie spoke!" he gasped. "He's not supposed to do that!"

The bang on the head had activated the speech-centre in Odie's brain.

"This is amazing," said Garfield. "I didn't think Odie had a brain!"

"What shall we talk about?" asked Odie.

"I'm easy," replied Garfield. "The ever-rising price of dog biscuits? Early Medieval latin?"

"I get latin when I whine at the door," said Odie.

"I can see this is going to be a stimulating conversation," murmured Garfield.

Odie made Garfield go outside.

"You think I'm stupid, don't you?" cried Odie.

"Whatever gives you that idea?" replied Garfield.

"I'm going to prove how clever I am by telling you something about everything we see," exclaimed Odie. "Look at the house."

"What about it?" asked Garfield.

"Jon built it of bricks so the Big Bad Wolf can't huff and puff and blow it all down," said Odie.

"Oh, boy," groaned Garfield.

Odie pointed to a passing bird.

"They can fly because the force of gravity keeps them up," he said.

Then a car drove by.

"That's a Ford," proclaimed Odie.

"Very good," admitted Garfield.

"It's called a Ford," added Odie, "because cars are expensive and some people can't afford them."

"Dogs <u>did</u> evolve from rocks," muttered Garfield.

At the end of half an hour, Garfield had had enough.

"I'm going for a nap, Odie," he called. "See you in a couple of years."

"Couldn't we play another game?" pleaded Odie.

"Like what?" said Garfield.

"Snakes and ladders," suggested Odie.

"Where am I going to get a boa constrictor?" asked Garfield.

"Hangman, then," cried Odie.

"I don't think Jon's got a rope," said Garfield.

In the end, they decided to play hide and seek.

"I'll hide," called Garfield, lying down in the middle of the room. "You close your eyes and count to ten."

"One . . . two . . . seven . . . four," said Odie. "No, that's not right. One . . . three . . . nine . . . two . . ."

"I've no chance of being found this side of Christmas," smiled Garfield, closing his eyes.

Suddenly, Odie spotted Jon's calculator lying in the corner. By pressing the numbers in turn, he managed to finish counting.

"Ready or not," he yelled, "here I come!"

Odie charged across the room and tripped over Garfield who was snoring on the floor. The startled dog flew through the air and hit the wall in exactly the same spot he had done earlier.

"Are you okay, Odie?" asked Garfield, opening one eye.

"Arf!" barked Odie.

"What did you say? cried Garfield, sitting up excitedly.

"Arf, arf, arf," repeated Odie.

"That's what I hoped you said," grinned Garfield.

Shortly afterwards, Jon came home. He found Garfield and Odie giving each other piggy-back rides. He clasped his hands together and watched his pets fondly.

"If only they could talk," he sighed.

Odie's Spiral Puzzle

Poor Odie! He's in a spin yet again! This time it's because he's been trying to work out this spiral puzzle. Perhaps you can help him. Solve the clues and write the answers in the grid. (Some go backwards.) The last letter of each answer also forms the first letter of the next.

Solution on page 61.

1. Heavyweight animal (8 letters)
2. Go brown in the sun (3 letters)
3. Mathematical amount (6 letters)
4. Competition to be first (4 letters)
5. King of the birds (5 letters)
6. Used for hearing (4 letters)
7. Goes under a cup (6 letters)

8. Glowing with light (7 letters)
9. Day after today (8 letters)
10. Rain, wind, snow and sun (7 letters)
11. Cook meat in oven (5 letters)
12. Little drum with bells, man! (10 letters)
13. Gain money by working (4 letters)

A CUDDLE CURES ANYTHING!

HI, THIS IS JON ARBUCKLE. MY CAT NEEDS A CHECKUP... WHAT KIND OF CAT IS HE?

UH, HE'S A REGISTERED YELLOW TABBY WITH DISTINGUISHED LINEAGE

© 1986 United Feature Syndicate, Inc.

ACTUALLY, HE'S AN ORANGE MEATBALL WITH STRIPES

JIM DAVIS   2-3

HEY, GARFIELD, LET'S GET A PIZZA!

JIM DAVIS 2-4

OH, NO!   HA HA!

SLAM!

© 1986 United Feature Syndicate, Inc.

ON THE WAY WE'LL STOP AT THE VET

IT'S THE OLD BAIT-AND-SWITCH!

A DOG CALLED GARFIELD

Last year, a dog called Raycroft Socialite became Supreme Champion at Crufts, the world's most prestigious dog show. Watched by millions on TV, the loveable Clumber Spaniel from the Irish Republic beat over 20,000 other contestants to become the first Irish dog ever to win this coveted title.

Raycroft Socialite is the dog's official show name. His real name is GARFIELD!

Star Of The Show

 Garfield's owner, Ralph Dunne, began to suspect he owned a superstar when, in his first year, Garfield won the Dublin Dog Show. His suspicions were confirmed shortly afterwards when his limelight-loving spaniel won the Pup of the Year Show in Manchester.

 The 100th Crufts Dog Show was held at the National Exhibition Centre in Birmingham. Garfield began by winning the Best Dog award in his class. Then he walked off with the title of Gundog Champion. Finally, he clinched the title of Supreme Champion. It was a breathtaking moment. Watching at home on TV, Ralph Dunne's mother said: "I just jumped for joy. I cried and cheered. It was incredible."

After the show, Garfield was whisked away to film a dog food commercial. Before his return to Ireland, he appeared on 'Blue Peter' where, despite the bright lights, he happily chomped his way through several pieces of bread. He is now back home in his kennel which he sleeps in every night, going for long walks with his master and romping in the mud like any other family pet.

Garfield is a great character. Says his owner: "I imagine he won Crufts because he's so full of character. He goes around the ring with great drive and purpose. He thoroughly enjoys performing."

Like his namesake, however, Garfield does not believe in wasting energy. When he was waiting to parade round the ring in front of the judges, he fell asleep and only just came to life when it was time to go into action!

WITH THAT NAME, THE GUY COULDN'T FAIL TO BE A CHAMP!

GARFIELD ON STAGE

In recent years, Garfield has presented his own Magic Show at nearly every major theatre in the country, including a Christmas season at the famous Mermaid Theatre in London. He has also appeared at numerous Shopping Precincts (Garfield would call them 'Malls') and Leisure Centres, as well as starring in major pantomimes alongside well-known TV personalities such as Paul Nicholas and Sue Pollard. Produced by Children's Showtime, The Garfield Magic Show continues to delight young audiences everywhere with a hilarious mixture of music, magic and fun.

Garfield's Show-Stoppers

During the show, Garfield performs a series of mind-boggling magic tricks. His favourite involves holding his top hat, saying the magic words "ABRACALASAGNE" and – hey presto – pulling out a giant lasagne by the ears.

Odie is Garfield's magical assistant. (As Garfield says, "small, insignificant parts" are best suited to Odie's limited talents.) In this role, Garfield insists that Odie wears a pink bow and a net ballet skirt, an outfit which never fails to bring the house down.

Odie's solo performance involves making some balloon animals. However, Garfield makes sure the supply of balloons is severely limited and is known to have burst many of Odie's finished masterpieces.

Garfield likes to encourage audience participation in his show. So he often asks an unsuspecting victim (sorry, volunteer) to come up on stage and appear on television. This involves wearing a box TV screen over the head which Garfield twists mercilessly to get a better picture!

The stars of the show relax on the golf course after another stunning performance.

 For a little exercise (not high on Garfield's list of priorities), his favourite game is called 'Chasing the Postman'. His second favourite game is building a tower of plastic buckets and metal trays. This is played by a girl's team versus a boy's team, but Garfield is fond of knocking the buckets down with a swish of his tail. End of game!

No show would be complete without the appearance of Pooky. Garfield decides his teddy needs a clean, having used him as a football on a muddy pitch. But Garfield's washing powder does not come from the local supermarket, and poor Pooky undergoes various colour washes and shrinks in boiling water before he is finally restored to a brighter-than-white (or, in his case, browner-than-brown) condition.

JON'S DOT~TO~DOT QUIZ

Jon's dress-sense may be zilch and his success with women zero-rated, but he knows a thing or two about drawing. (He is, after all, a cartoonist by profession.) So he's kindly come up with an unusual sort of quiz which will involve you in a little drawing and colouring yourself.

Here are 10 questions about famous cartoon characters. Each one you get right entitles you to fill in some of the dots on the picture opposite. When your picture is complete, you can colour it in. (Answers on page 61.)

DOTS 1-10
Who was Walt Disney's first cartoon character?
(a) Mickey Mouse
(b) Donald Duck
(c) Dumbo

DOTS 10-20
Who is 'strong to the finish' as a result of eating a certain type of greens?

DOTS 20-30
Which character in 'The Beano' has appeared since the first issue in 1938?
(a) Dennis the Menace
(b) Minnie the Minx
(c) Lord Snooty

DOTS 30-40
Bugs Bunny starred in 'Watership Down', the classic cartoon film about rabbits.
(a) True?
(b) False?

DOTS 40-50
What was the name of the cartoon film that featured The Beatles?
(a) Help!
(b) A Hard Day's Night
(c) Yellow Submarine

DOTS 50-60
Whose best friend is a little yellow bird called Woodstock?

DOTS 60-70
Who lives in Jellystone Park?
(a) Huckleberry Hound
(b) Yogi Bear
(c) Top Cat

DOTS 70-80
What type of character is Hägar the Horrible?
(a) A Viking
(b) A monster
(c) A spider

DOTS 80-90
Roy of the Rovers is a cartoon dog.
(a) True?
(b) False?

DOTS 90-100
Which famous cartoon family has a baby called Pebbles?
(a) The Simpsons
(b) The Flintstones
(c) Thundercats

IF YOU DON'T FEEL LIKE DOING THE QUIZ, JUST JOIN THE DOTS ANYWAY!

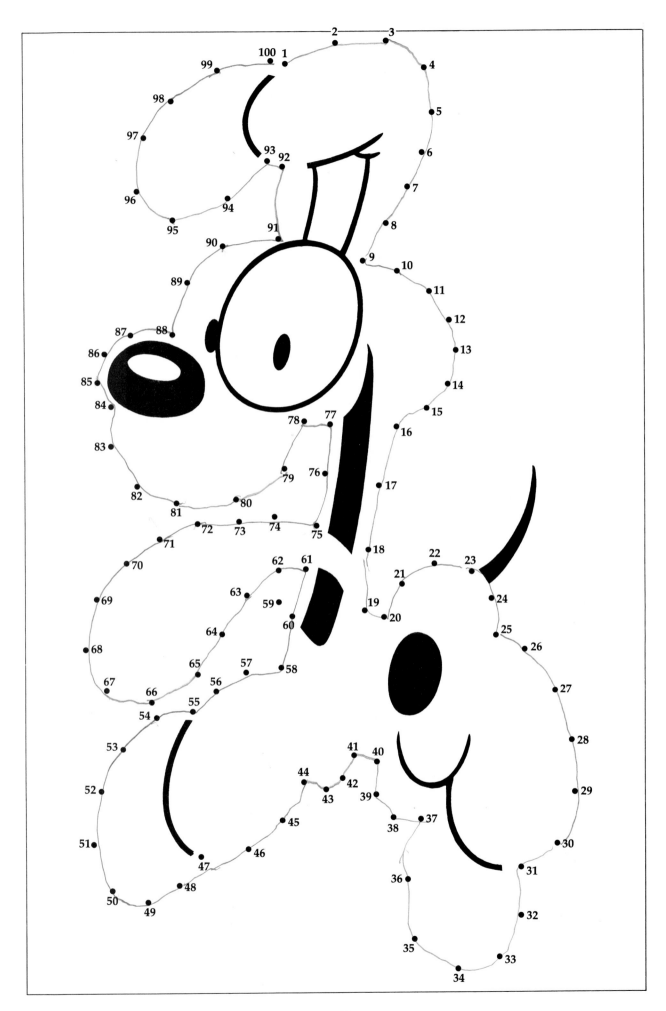

53

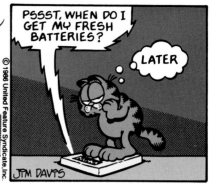

A LASAGNE A DAY
KEEPS THE DIET
AT BAY!

Garfield's Coded Joke

Use the code down the right-hand side of the page to decipher one of Garfield's favourite jokes. (Answers on page 61.)

23	8	1	20
W	H	A	T

4	9	4
D	I	D

20	8	5
T	H	E

3	1	20	5	18	16	9	12	12	1	18
C	A	T	E	R	P	I	L	L	A	R

19	1	25
S	A	Y

20	15
T	O

20	8	5
T	H	E

2	21	20	20	5	18	6	12	25	?
B	U	T	T	E	R	F	L	Y	?

25	15	21	'	12	12
Y	O	U	'	L	L

14	5	22	5	18
N	E	V	E	R

7	5	20
G	E	T

13	5
M	E

21	16
U	P

9	14
I	N

15	14	5
O	N	E

15	6
O	K

20	8	15	19	5
T	H	O	S	E

20	8	9	14	7	19	!
T	H	I	N	G	S	!

1	A
2	B
3	C
4	D
5	E
6	F
7	G
8	H
9	I
10	J
11	K
12	L
13	M
14	N
15	O
16	P
17	Q
18	R
19	S
20	T
21	U
22	V
23	W
24	X
25	Y
26	Z

A CUCKOO IN THE NESS

Picturepoint – London

"Someone's stolen our picnic, Garfield!" cried Jon.

"Don't look at me, pal," replied Garfield. "My stomach's as empty as Odie's head."

"It's a mystery, Garfield," continued Jon. "I left our picnic basket by the side of the loch and now it's empty!"

"Well, that's it," said Garfield, marching towards the car. "Let's head back for the bright lights!"

"Not so fast, Garfield," cried Jon, pulling his pet backwards. "We came here for a purpose and we're not leaving until we've seen it through!"

Garfield and Jon were visiting Scotland. Jon had heard that a scientific team was investigating Loch Ness and he wanted to be in on the action.

"I've brought my camcorder with me," he said, "and I'm going to be the first person to take a video of the Loch Ness monster. Imagine what a sensation that would cause!"

"Especially if you include a shot of your tartan trousers," added Garfield.

Jon strode round the banks of the loch, filming every little ripple in the water.

"Isn't this exciting, Garfield!" he exclaimed.

"Mind-blowing," muttered Garfield.

"Tell you what," continued Jon, lifting his cat up into a tree. "You can be lookout. Sit on that branch and give me a wave when Nessie rears his head up out of the water."

"The things I do for that man," grumbled Garfield. He hunched his shoulders and made himself look pathetic.

"A passing osprey might feel sorry for me and drop me a salmon," he murmured.

There were no fish eagles over the loch today. There was no sign of the monster lurking beneath it, either. In fact, there was nothing to see at all except an endless expanse of grey water beneath an endless expanse of grey sky.

"Haven't been so bored since the TV broke down," growled Garfield. He tried to settle down for a nap, but the biting Highland wind kept him awake.

"When can I get down?" he yelled, tapping his wrists to ask Jon about the time.

"Stay there for about 5 or 6 hours," called Jon, hurrying off to film a log in the water.

"That's longer than it takes Odie to write his name," groaned Garfield.

To keep warm, Garfield began to exercise. He opened and closed his eyes several times, scratched behind his ear and stretched one leg out behind him. Then he went for the big one, hanging upside down by his feet.

"This place doesn't look any different this way up," he commented. Garfield was just about to swing upright again when there was a loud CRACK!

"I'm heading for the ground floor without a lift!" he yelled. Luckily, Jon had chosen this tree because it leaned out from the shore, so Garfield landed in the water. The gigantic splash sent shock-waves along the entire 36 kilometers of the loch.

Garfield plummeted down into the murky darkness beneath the waves.

"I'm glad you've dropped in," said a deep, booming voice. "I've got a bone to pick with you."

Garfield peered through the gloom and a huge face loomed up at him, showing teeth the size of tombstones.

"Nessie!" gasped Garfield.

"None other!" replied the monster.

"How can I help you?" asked Garfield, deciding politeness was the best way to handle this fearsome-looking creature.

"That lasagne I took from your picnic gave me indigestion," grumbled Nessie, emitting a rumble burp that echoed through the water like thunder.

"I'll get you something from the chemist . . ." began Garfield.

"No need," replied the monster, heading Garfield off. "I want something else to settle my tum. Something more solid. Something like YOU!"

With that, Nessie opened his gigantic mouth. Garfield swam for his life.

"This guy makes Jaws look like a tadpole," he gulped.

Garfield expended more energy during the next ten minutes than in the rest of his life put together. He just managed to keep his back feet a few centimetres in front of the gnashing teeth. Suddenly, Nessie gave up.

"Nice meeting you, lardball," called Garfield, watching the great beast sinking back into the depths.

Garfield looked around. He hoped to see Jon waiting for him with a fluffy towel and an emergency bar of chocolate, but the shore was almost out of sight.

"Oh, terrific," groaned Garfield. "I've swum right out to the middle of the loch."

Garfield felt too tired to swim back immediately, so he spread his arms and legs out wide and floated on his back.

"With a bit of imagination," he murmured, "this could be a water-bed."

Back on shore, Jon had met up with the scientists investigating Loch Ness. They were in a state of high excitement.

"Our equipment has detected intense underwater activity," one explained.

"That must mean the monster's on the move," exclaimed Jon. "I wonder if Garfield's spotted him?"

Jon hurried back towards the look-out tree. Half-way there, he stopped dead in his tracks. Peering out towards the middle of the loch, he could just make out a huge, rounded shape bobbing up and down in the water.

"It's Nessie!" he gasped.

Jon switched on his camcorder and pointed it in the direction of the sighting. The camera whirred for a moment or two, then cut out.

"OH, NO!" wailed Jon. "I've used up all my tape!"

By the time he had loaded another cassette, the creature had gone.

"I'd better not tell Garfield I've missed the chance of a lifetime," murmured Jon.

Mention of Garfield made Jon realise he had not seen his pet for a long time. He ran back to the tree and was dismayed not to find Garfield still on the branch. Then a bedraggled figure emerged from the water, spitting out mouthfuls of weed and glaring like an African war-mask.

"Oh, Garfield!" exclaimed Jon, feeling overcome with guilt. "You got so hungry, you went in fishing! How can I make it up to you?"

"Buy me a pizza factory," said Garfield.

Jon took Garfield back to town. Garfield celebrated his return to civilisation by making a whistle-stop tour of every burger bar within a hundred kilometre radius. Afterwards, he sat and watched Jon's video of their visit to Loch Ness.

"It's even more boring than the real thing," muttered Garfield. Jon woke his cat up when the tape finished.

"I have a confession to make, Garfield" said Jon. "I saw the monster but I missed filming it. The thing was out at the middle of the lake – a sort of orangey colour, huge and really HIDEOUS!"

"Cheers, Jon," said Garfield.

Home Sweet Home Quiz
(pages 16 and 17)

1. Heart
2. (a) Golden eagle
3. (a) Otter
4. Sherlock Holmes
5. King Arthur
6. (c) The Chancellor of the Exchequer
7. (b) Mount Olympus
8. Liverpool – Anfield
   Tottenham Hotspur – White Hart Lane
   Arsenal – Highbury
   Manchester United – Old Trafford
   Leeds United – Elland Road
   Southampton – The Dell
9. (a) Dad's Army
10. Nomads
11. A rabbit burrow is a single underground home; a rabbit warren is a large collection of burrows connected by tunnels.
12. (a) William the Conqueror
13. (b) Henry the Eighth
14. Robinson Crusoe
15. The old lady who lived in a shoe
16. Oliver Twist
17. (b) False. 'Heimat' is the German word for 'home'. In Spanish, it is 'casa'
18. (b) Badger
19. (b) False. Aboriginees are the native people of Australia. The Maoris live in New Zealand
20. (a) Hubert and Reba

Garfield's Traditional Dish Puzzle *(page 26)*

PIZZA – ITALY
PAELLA – SPAIN
HAGGIS – SCOTLAND
CHOP SUEY – CHINA
SNAILS – FRANCE
CURRY – INDIA
MOUSSAKA – GREECE
FISH AND CHIPS – ENGLAND
CHILLI CON CARNE – MEXICO
SUSHI (Raw Fish) – JAPAN
HAMBURGERS – AMERICA
SAUERKRAUT – GERMANY

Arlene's Arroword *(page 34)*

TINY INSECT	A	N	T	R	BABY'S BED	C	O	T	E
BORN IN THE USA	M	THINGS FOR CARRYING FOOD	R	FUNNY DRAWINGS OF FILM	A	LIVE IN RENTED HOUSES	E	
PERIOD OF TIME	E	R	A	MOVE FAST	R	U	N	
	B	R	A	Y	DONKEY NOISE	T		A
SHORT FOR 'IT IS'	I	T	S	TO POSSESS	O	W	N	
	A	C	E	PUT IN ORDER	S	O	R	T
GOOD AT FLYING OR TENNIS		A	DEGREE OF SPEED	B	O	N	E	S
	N		PARTS OF SKELETON	B	L	CRY LOUDLY	N	L	TINY BIRD

Odie's Spiral Puzzle *(page 38)*

Jon's Dot-To-Dot Quiz *(pages 48 and 49)*

Dots 1-10
(a) Mickey Mouse
Dots 11-20 Popeye
Dots 21-30
(c) Lord Snooty
Dots 31-40   (b) False
Dots 41-50
(c) Yellow Submarine
Dots 51-60 Snoopy
Dots 61-70
(b) Yogi Bear
Dots 71-80
(a) A Viking
Dots 81-90   (b) False
(He is a footballer)
Dots 91-100
(b) The Flintstones

Garfield's Coded Joke *(page 56)*

WHAT DID THE CATERPILLAR SAY TO THE BUTTERFLY?

YOU'LL NEVER GET ME UP IN ONE OF THOSE THINGS!